G. SCHIRMER'
COLLECTION O
OPERA LIBRETTOS

CAVALLERIA RUSTICANA

Opera in One Act

Music by
Pietro Mascagni

Libretto by
G. TARGIONI-TOZZETTI and G. MENASCI
After a story by Giovanni Verga

English Version by
JOSEPH MACHLIS

Ed. 2532

G. SCHIRMER, Inc.

CAVALLERIA RUSTICANA

Pietro Mascagni (1863-1945) was born in the Italian seaport of Livorno (Leghorn), the son of a baker. His father intended him to become a lawyer and bitterly opposed his musical studies, whereupon a sympathetic uncle adopted the boy and encouraged him in his artistic endeavors. Mascagni studied at the Conservatory of Milan. But, chafing under academic routine, he left school in the middle of his course and spent several years as a conductor of traveling opera companies

He was twenty-six years old and deeply discouraged about his career as a composer when he entered his one-act opera *Cavalleria rusticana* (Rustic Chivalry) in a contest sponsored by the Milan publisher Sonzogno. The work not only won first prize but catapulted Mascagni into international fame. In the course of his long life he produced fourteen other operas, among them *L'amico Fritz* and *Iris;* but he never duplicated his first success. For the world he remains the creator of *Cavalleria.*

Based on a moving short story by the Sicilian novelist Giovanni Verga, Mascagni's masterpiece exemplifies the trend toward realism — known as *verismo* — that came to the fore in Italy in the late nineteenth century. The movement impelled operatic composers to draw their subjects from the life of the common people instead of concentrating on the affairs of kings and duchesses; and to treat these in simple down-to-earth fashion, with swift action and powerful — often violent — emotion. Leoncavallo's *Pagliacci* and Puccini's *Il tabarro* stand alongside *Cavalleria* as outstanding examples of this new realism in the Italian lyric theater.

Cavalleria received its premiere on May 17, 1890, at the Costanzi Theater in Rome. The work was heard for the first time in America at the Philadelphia Grand Opera on September 9, 1891, and reached the Metropolitan Opera House three months later, when it was presented with Emma Eames as Santuzza and Fernando Valero as Turiddu.

J. M.

THE STORY

The action takes place on Easter Day in a Sicilian village. Turiddu is heard offstage singing a serenade to Lola, the pretty wife of the prosperous carter Alfio. The villagers, in holiday attire, hymn the spring. After they leave, Santuzza enters in great agitation and approaches the tavern of Mamma Lucia. She is looking for her lover Turiddu, Lucia's son.

Alfio appears with his companions. His jolly song reveals not only his manly nature but also his happiness with his wife and his joy in the vigorous life of a carter. The villagers intone a hymn to the Savior and enter the church. Now Santuzza reveals to Lucia that Turiddu, after having loved her for a time, has abandoned her and gone back to his former sweetheart, Lola. Mamma Lucia is shocked by the tidings. She goes to Mass. When Turiddu appears, Santuzza begs him to come back to her but he turns a deaf ear to her pleading. Lola comes by on her way to church. A natural coquette, she makes no effort to conceal her contempt for Santuzza and her power over Turiddu. She enters the church; Turiddu wants to follow her. Santuzza tries to hold him back but only arouses him to fury. He throws her aside and runs into the church. Santuzza, beside herself with rage, curses him.

When Alfio returns, Santuzza reveals the truth to him. The betrayed husband rushes off, vowing to be avenged. At this point the famous Intermezzo introduces a note of peace and revery into the gathering tragedy. The villagers come from church. Turiddu invites them to the tavern for a holiday drink. All join him in a lively drinking song. He lifts his glass in a toast to Lola. Alfio arrives; Turiddu pours him a glass of wine which the carter scornfully refuses. Sensing that a quarrel is about to break out, the villagers withdraw, taking Lola with them.

Turiddu, left alone with Alfio, admits his guilt. The two Sicilians realize that the affair can be settled in only one way. Alfio promises to wait for Turiddu behind the orchard. Alone with his mother, Turiddu bids her a tender farewell and implores her to take care of Santuzza in the event he should not return. Mamma Lucia is bewildered by his words. He blames his mood on the wine, tells her he is going for a walk to clear his head, and leaves. Santuzza rushes in, distraught, and throws her arms around Lucia. Shouting is heard in the distance. Soon women come rushing into the square with the news that Turiddu has been killed.

CAST OF CHARACTERS

SANTUZZA, a peasant girl . . . . Soprano

LUCIA, mother of Turiddu . . . . Contralto

ALFIO, a village teamster . . . . Baritone

TURIDDU, a soldier, son of Lucia . . . . Tenor

LOLA, wife of Alfio . . . . Mezzo-soprano

Villages and Peasants.

PLACE: A Sicilian village

TIME: Nineteenth century

CAVALLERIA RUSTICANA

La scena rappresenta una piazza in un paese della Sicilia. Nel fondo, a destra, Chiesa con porta praticabile. A sinistra l'osteria e la casa di Mamma Lucia. È il giorno di Pasqua.

TURIDDU (*sipario calato*)

O Lola, bianca come fior di spino,
Quando t'affacci tu, s'affaccia il sole;
Chi t' ha baciato il labbro porporino
Grazia più bella a Dio chieder non
  vôle.
C'è scritto sangue sopra la tua porta,
Ma di restarci a me non me n'importa;
Se per te mojo e vado in paradiso,
Non c'entro se non vedo il tuo bel viso.

CORO DONNE (*di dentro*)

Gli aranci olezzano
Sui verdi margini,
Gli augelli cantano
Tra i mirti in fior;
Tempo è si mormori
Da orgnuno il tenero
Canto che i palpiti
Raddoppia al cor.

UOMINI (*di dentro*).

In mezzo al campo tra le spiche d'oro
Giunge il rumore delle vostre spole,
Noi stanchi riposando dal lavoro
A voi pensiamo, o belle occhi-di-sole.
O belle occhi-di-sole, a voi corriamo,
Come vola l'augello al suo richiamo.

(*Il coro entra in iscena.*)

DONNE

Cessin le rustiche
Opre: la Vergine
Serena allietasi
Del Salvator;

Tempo è si mormori
Da ognuno il tenero
Canto che i palpiti
Raddoppia al cor.

(*Il coro traversa la scena ed esce.*)

SANTUZZA (*entrando*)
Dite, mamma Lucia . . .

LUCIA (*sorpresa*)
Sei tu? . . . che vuoi?

SANTUZZA
Turiddu ov'è?

LUCIA
Fin qui vieni a cercare
Il figlio mio?

SANTUZZA
Voglio saper soltanto,
Perdonatemi voi, dove trovarlo.

LUCIA
Non lo so, non lo so, non voglio brighe!

SANTUZZA
Mamma Lucia, vi supplico piangendo,
Fate come il Signore a Maddalena,
Ditemi per pietà, dov'è Turiddu?

LUCIA
È andato per il vino a Francofonte.

SANTUZZA
No! l'han visto in paese ad alta notte.

LUCIA
Che dici? se non è tornato a casa!
Entra!

SANTUZZA (*disperata*)
Non posso entrare in casa vostra,
Sono scomunicata!

LUCIA
E che ne sai
Del mio figliuolo?

SANTUZZA
Quale spina ho in core!

(*Entrano Alfio e Coro*)

1

CAVALLERIA RUSTICANA

*A public square in a Sicilian village.
At the back, on the left, is a church.
On the right is the cottage and tav-
ern of Mamma Lucia. The time is
Easter Day.*

*(As the curtain rises Turiddu is heard
singing outside.)*

TURIDDU

Oh, Lola, my beloved, fair as a flower,
How I adore your smile, brighter than
    sunlight!
Lips that are scarlet red, glowing with
    passion,
Bring me the pleasures of heaven when
    I caress them!
If I could know my fate, oh my be-
    loved . . .
Know that my soul was doomed to suf-
    fer forever,
Yet would I seek your love, though it
    destroy me . . .
Suffer the pain and sorrow if you were
    near me!
Though I were doomed to die, die for
    my Lola,
Yet would I suffer gladly if you were
    near me!

WOMEN *(offstage)*

See how the orange is
Blossoming everywhere!
Birds in the field,
And the meadows in flower!
Brightly the marigolds
Blossoming everywhere,
Song of the nightingale
Fills every bower.

MEN *(offstage)*

A drowsy silence fills the meadow;
We hear your merry voices in the twi-
    light.
How pleasant to rest from our labor!
We think of you with endless joy and
    longing!
Oh lovely women, we hasten, eager to
    find you,
As a bird who is homing seeks his be-
    loved.

WOMEN

Planting and sowing are over.
The angelus is ringing,
Announcing the end of our toil.
Welcome the gentle spring,

Season of tender enchantment
When hearts rejoice.
Happy time of love!
*(The peasants cross the scene and go
off.)*

SANTUZZA *(enters)*

Tell me, Mamma Lucia—

LUCIA *(surprised)*

It's you! What is it?

SANTUZZA

Where is Turiddu?

LUCIA

Turiddu?
Why do you want to see my son?

SANTUZZA

Tell me the truth, I beg you!
I must speak with Turiddu.
Where can I find him?

LUCIA

Don't ask me, I want no trouble!

SANTUZZA

Mamma Lucia! With bitter tears I beg
    you.
Even Mary Magdalene found mercy!
Tell me, in heaven's name, where is
    Turiddu!

LUCIA

He's gone to bring the wine from
    Francofonte.

SANTUZZA

No! Last night someone saw him in
    the village.

LUCIA

Who said so? Who told you?
Surely they must be mistaken!
Come in, then!

SANTUZZA *(in dispair)*

Mamma Lucia, do not ask me.
I cannot enter, I'm nothing but a sin-
    ner, nothing but an outcast.

LUCIA

Is my Turiddu in any trouble?

SANTUZZA

I don't know how to tell you . . .
(Enter Alfio and people of the village.)

1

ALFIO

Il cavallo scalpita,
I sonagli squillano,
Schiocca la frusta. Ehi là!
Soffi il vento gelido,
Cada l'acqua e nevichi,
A me che cosa fa?

CORO

O che bel mestiere
Fare il carrettiere
Andar di quà e di là!

ALFIO

M'aspetta a casa Lola
Che m'ama e mi consola,
Ch'è tutta fedeltà.
Il cavallo scalpita,
I sonagli squillano,
È Pasqua, ed io son quà!

CORO

O che bel mestiere
Fare il carrettiere
Andar di quà e di là.

LUCIA

Beato voi, compar Alfio, che siete sempre allegro così!

ALFIO

Mamma Lucia,
N'avete ancora di quel vecchio vino?

LUCIA

Non so; Turiddu è andato a provvederne.

ALFIO

Se è sempre qui! L'ho visto stamattina vicino a casa mia.

LUCIA *(sorpresa)*

Come?

SANTUZZA *(rapidamente)*

Tacete.
(dalla Chiesa odesi intonare l'alleluja)

ALFIO

Io me ne vado, ite voi altri in chiesa.
(esce)

CORO INTERNO
(dalla chiesa)

Regina cœli, lætare—Alleluja!
Quia, quem meruisti portare—Alleluja!
Resurrexit sicut dixit—Alleluja!

CORO ESTERNO
(sulla piazza)

Inneggiamo, il Signor non è morto,
Ei fulgente ha dischiuso l'avel,
Inneggiamo al Signore risorto
Oggi asceso alla gloria del Ciel'

CORO INTERNO
(dalla chiesa)

Ora pro nobis Deum—Alleluja!
Gaude et lætare, Virgo Maria—Alleluja!
Quia surrexit Dominus vere—Alleluja!

CORO ESTERNO
(sulla piazza)

Dall' altare ora fu benedetto
Quest' olivo che amava il Signor;
Porti e accresca nell'umile tetto
La domestica pace e l'amor!
(Il coro esce lentamente.)

LUCIA

Perchè m'hai fatto segno di tacere?

SANTUZZA

Voi lo sapete, o mamma, prima d'andar soldato
Turiddu aveva a Lola eterna fè giurato.
Tornò, la seppe sposa; a con un nuovo amore
Volle spegner la fiamma che gli bruciava il core:
M'amò, l'amai. Quell'invidia d'ogni delizia mia,
Del suo sposo dimentica, arse di gelosia.
Me l'ha rapito. Priva dell'onor mio rimango:
Lola e Turiddu s'amano, io piango, io piango!

LUCIA

Miseri noi, che cosa vieni a dirmi
In questo santo giorno?

SANTUZZA

Io son dannata.
Andate, o mamma, ad implorare Iddio,
E pregate per me. Verrà Turiddu,
Vo' supplicarlo un'altra volta ancora!

ALFIO

Horse and wagon dash along,
Silver bells in merry song,
Crack of the whip—and away!
What if winter wind should blow?
What care I for wind or snow?
Always a happy day!

CHORUS

Merrily he's singing,
Silver bells are ringing,
He travels far and wide!

ALFIO

My Lola is a treasure,
Our life is joy and pleasure,
She is my faithful love.
My Lola is a beauty,
She knows her wifely duty,
She is my little dove.
It's Easter and I am home at last!

CHORUS

Merrily he's singing,
Silver bells are ringing
He travels far and wide,
He's on his merry way!

LUCIA

You are lucky, dear Alfio!
You're always so contented, so gay!

ALFIO

Mamma Lucia,
Did you receive the wine you were
expecting?

LUCIA

Not yet. Turiddu is on his way to buy
some.

ALFIO

But he's still here. This morning, very
early, I saw him near my house.

LUCIA (surprised)
Really?

SANTUZZA (quickly)
Be quiet.
(music from the church)

ALFIO

I'd better hurry, I must get ready for
church.
(He leaves.)

CHORUS
(from the church)
Regina Coeli, laetare—Alleluja!
Quia, quem meruisti portare—Alleluja!
Resurrexit sicut dixit—Allelujah!

CHORUS
(on the square)
Let us sing to our Father in heaven,
Praise the Lord in his splendor and
might!
Let us sing and rejoice, Christ is risen,
And ascends into glory and light!

CHORUS
(from the church)
Ora pro nobis Deum—Alleluja!
Gaude et laetare, Virgo Maria—
Alleluja!
Quia surrexit Dominus vere—Alleluja!

CHORUS
(on the square)
Let us sing to our Father in heaven,
Let us sing to His Son who is risen,
Lord of mercy and love,
Prince of peace and joy
Who this day ascends into glory and
light!
(The chorus slowly leaves the scene.)

LUCIA

But why did you tell me to be silent?

SANTUZZA

Don't you remember, Mamma, when
he became a soldier,
Turiddu loved only Lola, thought they
would soon be married,
And hoped to find great happiness
forever.
He returned. Lola was married.
Turridu turned to me in sorrow,
Tried to forget his passion:
He loved me, I loved him.
She envied the joy I found.
She was faithless to Alfio;
Burning with spiteful envy, she stole
Turiddu.
Robbed of love and honor, I am alone
and abandoned:
Lola and Turiddu . . . lovers again. I
weep alone.

LUCIA

Father in heaven! What dreadful things
to tell me this holy Easter morning.

SANTUZZA

I'm cursed forever!
I beg you, Mamma, to pray for my sal-
vation.
Mama, pray for my soul!
I'll see Turiddu and I will try to move
his heart to pity.

LUCIA (*avviandosi alla chiesa*)
Ajutatela voi, Santa Maria!
(*esce*)

TURIDDU
(*entra*)
Tu qui, Santuzza?

SANTUZZA
Qui t'aspettavo.

TURIDDU
È Pasqua, in chiesa non vai?

SANTUZZA
Non vo.
Debbo parlarti.

TURIDDU
Mamma cercavo.

SANTUZZA
Debbo parlarti!

TURIDDU
Qui no! Qui no!

SANTUZZA
Dove sei stato?

TURIDDU
Che vuoi tu dire?
A Francofonte!

SANTUZZA
No, non è ver!

TURIDDU
Santuzza, credimi.

SANTUZZA
No, non mentire;
Ti vidi volgere giù dal sentier.
E stamattina, all' alba, t'hanno scôrto
Presso l'uscio di Lola.

TURIDDU
Ah! m'hai spiato!

SANTUZZA
No, te lo giuro. A noi l'ha raccontato
Compar Alfio, il marito, poco fa.

TURIDDU
Così ricambi l'amor che ti porto?
Vuoi che m'uccida?

SANTUZZA
Oh! questo non lo dire—

TURIDDU
Lasciami dunque, invan tenti sopire
Il giusto sdegno colla tua pietà.

SANTUZZA
Tu l'ami dunque?

TURIDDU
No!

SANTUZZA
Assai più bella è Lola.

TURIDDU
Taci, non l'amo.

SANTUZZA
L'ami, l'ami,
Oh! maledetta!

TURIDDU
Santuzza!

SANTUZZA
Quella cattiva femmina ti tolse a me!

TURIDDU
Bada, Santuzza, schiavo non sono
Di questa vana tua gelosia!

SANTUZZA
Battimi, insultami, t'amo e perdono,
Ma è troppo forte l'angoscia mia.

LOLA (*dentro alla scena*)
Fior di giaggiolo,
Gli angeli belli stanno a mille in cielo,
Ma bello come lui ce n'è uno solo.
(*entrando*)
Oh! Turiddu, è passato Alfio?

TURIDDU
(*impacciato*)
Son giunto ora in piazza. Non so.

LOLA
Forse è rimasto dal maniscalco, ma non
può tardare.
(*ironica*)
E voi sentite le funzioni in piazza?

TURIDDU
Santuzza mi narrava . . .

LUCIA
May the Virgin help you. O blessed
Mother!

(*She enters the church.*)

TURIDDU (*enters*)
You here, Santuzza?

SANTUZZA
I want to see you.

TURIDDU
Why don't you go to church, Santuzza?

SANTUZZA
I can't! I have to see you.

TURIDDU
Where is my mother?

SANTUZZA
I have to see you.

TURIDDU
Not now . . . not now!

SANTUZZA
Where have you been?

TURIDDU
Where have I been?
To Francofonte.

SANTUZZA
No . . . that's a lie!

TURIDDU
You must believe me . . .

SANTUZZA
No, you are lying!
I saw you come from the path by the
hill.
Will you deny you went to Lola's house
Very early this morning?

TURIDDU
Ah! You've been spying!

SANTUZZA
No! I swear it! It's Alfio who said it.
You were seen by the husband you
deceive!

TURIDDU
Is this the way you repay my devotion?
You want him to kill me?

SANTUZZA
Oh, how can you believe it?

TURIDDU
Leave me, Santuzza! Leave me now.
Don't ask me to forgive you.
I can't forget the things that you have
said.

SANTUZZA
Ah, then you love her?

TURIDDU
No!

SANTUZZA
I can't compete with Lola.

TURIDDU
Stop it, Santuzza!

SANTUZZA
You love her!
Oh, I could kill you!

TURIDDU
Santuzza!

SANTUZZA
Lola, that scheming creature, robbed
me of your love!

TURIDDU
Careful, Santuzza, I'm not your
slave . . .
I will not endure your hateful
suspicion!

SANTUZZA
Beat me, insult me, and still I will
love you!
I cannot bear this fearful torture.

LOLA (*offstage*)
My lovely flower!
Angels in heaven, robed in all their
splendor,
Cannot compare with you in charm or
beauty!
(*enters*)
Oh, Turiddu! Have you seen Alfio?

TURIDDU (*impatiently*)
Have I seen Alfio? Not today.

LOLA
Maybe he waited to see the blacksmith.
He'll be here any moment.
(*ironically*)
And you . . . you're holding a little
private service?

TURIDDU
Santuzza was just saying—

SANTUZZA (*tetra*)

Gli dicevo che oggi è Pasqua e il Signor
vede ogni cosa!

LOLA (*ironica*)

Non venite alla messa?

SANTUZZA (*tetra*)

Io no, ci deve andar chi sa di non aver
peccato.

LOLA

Io ringrazio il Signore e bacio in terra!

SANTUZZA (*ironica*)

Oh! fate bene, Lola!

TURIDDU

Andiamo! andiamo!
Qui non abbiam che fare.

LOLA (*ironica*)

Oh! rimanete!

SANTUZZA (*a Turiddu*)

Sì, resta, resta, ho da parlarti ancora!

LOLA

E v' assista il Signore, io me ne vado.
(*entra in chiesa*)

TURIDDU (*irato*)

Ah! lo vedi, che hai tu detto?

SANTUZZA

L'hai voluto, e ben ti sta.

TURIDDU (*le s'avventa*)

Ah! per Dio!

SANTUZZA

Squarciami il petto.

TURIDDU (*s'avvia*)

No!

SANTUZZA (*trattenendolo*)

Turiddu, ascolta!

TURIDDU

Va!

SANTUZZA

No, no, Turiddu, rimani ancora,
Abbandonarmi dunque tu vuoi?

TURIDDU

Perchè seguirmi, perchè spiarmi
Sul limitare fin della chiesa?

SANTUZZA

La tua Santuzza piange e t'implora;
Come cacciarla così tu puoi?

TURIDDU

Va, ti ripeto, va non tediarmi,
Pentirsi è vano dopo l'offesa.

SANTUZZA (*minacciosa*)

Bada!

TURIDDU

Dell' ira tua non mi curo!
(*la getta a terra e fugge in chiesa*)

SANTUZZA (*nel colmo dell'ira*)

A te la mala Pasqua, spergiuro!
(*Alfio entra.*)
Oh! il Signore vi manda, compar Alfio.

ALFIO

A che punto è la messa?

SANTUZZA

È tardi omai, ma per voi: Lola è
andata con Turiddu!

ALFIO

Che avete detto?

SANTUZZA

Che mentre correte all'acqua e al vento
a guadagnarvi il pane,
Lola v' adorna il tetto in malo modo!

ALFIO

Ah! nel nome di Dio, Santa, che dite?

SANTUZZA

Il ver. Turiddu mi tolse l'onore,
E vostra moglie lui rapiva a me!

ALFIO

Se voi mentite, vo' schiantarvi il core!

SANTUZZA (*gloomily*)
On this holy Easter morning
God is watching every sinner.

LOLA (*ironically*)
You're not going to Mass?

SANTUZZA (*sadly*)
I'm not. No one should go but those
who know they are not sinful.

LOLA
I am grateful to Heaven that I can
enter.

SANTUZZA (*ironically*)
Oh, you're so clever, Lola!

TURIDDU
Let's go then,
Or we will miss the service.

LOLA (*ironically*)
Oh . . . you can stay here!

SANTUZZA
Yes, stay here! There's something I
must tell you.

LOLA
May the Lord protect you.
I must be going.
(*She enters the church.*)

TURIDDU (*angrily*)
Now I see it. Very clever!

SANTUZZA
I'm not sorry. It serves you right!

TURIDDU (*threateningly*)
Oh, by Heaven!

SANTUZZA
Listen, Turiddu!

TURIDDU (*turns away*)
No!

SANTUZZA (*holding him back*)
Turiddu, I beg you!

TURIDDU
Go!

SANTUZZA
No, no Turiddu! Oh, do not forsake
me,
I beg you! Do not abandon me so
cruelly.

TURIDDU
Must you pursue me? Must you tor-
ment me?
Why must you spy on me every moment?

SANTUZZA
Ah, see your Santuzza humbly implor-
ing you.
How can you leave me, knowing I love
you?

TURIDDU
Leave me, Santuzza! Nothing you can
say
Would make me forgive you!

SANTUZZA (*threatening*)
I warn you!

TURIDDU
I've had enough of all your madness!
(*He throws her down and rushes into
the church.*)

SANTUZZA (*in the height of anger*)
My curse on you, Turiddu! Betrayer!

(*Alfio enters.*)
Oh! God Himself has sent you, neighbor Alfio.

ALFIO
Am I late for the service?

SANTUZZA
It's almost over. I must tell you . . .
Lola is there with Turiddu!

ALFIO
What's that you're saying?

SANTUZZA
That while you are working, while you
are slaving tò earn an honest living,
Lola was thinking only of Turiddu.

ALFIO
Ah! By all that is holy, what are you
saying?

SANTUZZA
The truth. Turiddu had promised he
always would love me.
Then he betrayed me!
And it was Lola who stole his love from
me.

ALFIO
If you are lying, I swear that I will kill
you!

SANTUZZA

Uso a mentire il labbro mio non è!
Per la vergogna mia, pel mio dolore
La trista verità vi dissi, ahimè!

ALFIO

Comare Santa, allor grato vi sono.

SANTUZZA

Infame io son che vi parlai così!

ALFIO

Infami loro! Ad essi non perdono,
Vendetta avrò pria che tramonti il dì.
Io sangue voglio, all' ira m'abbandono,
In odio tutto l'amor mio finì!

(*escono*)

INTERMEZZO

(*Tutti escono di chiesa. Lucia traversa
la scena ed entra in casa.*)

UOMINI

A casa, a casa, amici, ove ci aspettano
Le nostre donne, andiam.
Or che letizia rasserena gli animi
Senza indugio corriam.

DONNE

A casa, a casa, amiche, ove ci aspettano
I nostri sposi, andiam.
Or che letizia rasserena gli animi
Senza indugio corriam.

TURIDDU (*a Lola che s'avvia*)

Comare Lola, ve ne andate via
Senza nemmeno salutare?

LOLA

Vado a casa: non ho visto compar
Alfio!

TURIDDU

Non ci pensate, verrà in piazza.

(*al Coro*)

Intanto amici, qua, beviamone un
bicchiere.

(*tutti si avvicinano alla tavola dell'osteria
e prendono i bicchieri*)

Viva il vino spumeggiante
Nel bicchiere scintillante
Come il riso dell' amante
Mite infonde il giubilo!
Viva il vino ch' è sincero
Che ci allieta ogni pensiero,
E che affoga l'umor nero
Nell' ebbrezza tenera.

CORO (*si ripete*)
TURIDDU (*a Lola*)

Ai vostri amori! (*beve*)

LOLA (*a Turiddu*)

Alla fortuna vostra!

(*beve*)

TURIDDU

Beviam!

CORO

Beviam! Rinnovisi la giostra!

PRIMO DEL CORO

Un bicchiere!

SECONDO DEL CORO

Un bicchiere!

TERZO DEL CORO

Un altro!

QUARTO DEL CORO

Un altro!

PRIMO DEL CORO

Al più felice!

TURIDDU

Alla bella!

LOLA

Al più scaltro!

TUTTI

Viva il vino spumeggiante, ecc.

ALFIO

A voi tutti salute!

CORO

Compar Alfio, salute!

TURIDDU

Benevenuto! con noi dovete bere:
(*empie un bicchiere*)
Ecco, pieno è il bicchiere.

SANTUZZA

What have I to gain if I deceived you?
I swear by my terrible sorrow and
shame, as God is my witness!

ALFIO

Neighbor Santuzza, I'm grateful that
you told me.

SANTUZZA

I know it's sinful that I spoke like this.

ALFIO

They have betrayed me!
They'll pay for my dishonor!
I'll be revenged this very day.
My love has turned into bitter hate!
I swear to God that they will pay for
this!

(*They go out.*)

INTERMEZZO

(*The people come out of the church.
Lucia goes into her house.*)

MEN

Good neighbors, good neighbors, we
greet you!
We'll soon be home again.
Our wives are waiting, so come,
And let's enjoy this day of rest and
pleasure,
And good holiday cheer!

WOMEN

Good neighbors, good neighbors, we
greet you!
We'll soon be home again.
Our men are waiting, so come,
And let's enjoy this day of rest and
pleasure,
And good holiday cheer!

TURIDDU (*to Lola, who is leaving*)

Good neighbor Lola, do not leave so
quickly.
Come . . . here are friends who want
to greet you.

LOLA

I am going. I am looking for Alfio!

TURIDDU

You needn't worry, he'll be here soon.

(*to the people*)

My friends, come one and all!
Let's drink a toast to pleasure.
(*All go to the tables of the tavern and
take up glasses.*)
Merrily the wine is flowing,
Every heart is set a-glowing.
Love itself is more delightful
When we drink . . . so drain your glass!
Glorious wine, we hail your power!
Who would miss this precious hour?
Banish every care and sorrow!
Life and love are wonderful!

CHORUS (*repeats*)

TURIDDU (*to Lola*)

To your admirers! (*drinks*)

LOLA (*to Turiddu*)

And here's to your good fortune!
(*drinks*)

TURIDDU

Your health!

CHORUS

It's time we had another!

ONE OF THE CHORUS

We drink!

ANOTHER OF THE CHORUS

We drink!

A THIRD

To love!

A FOURTH

To life!

THE FIRST

Life is bright . . .

TURIDDU

Life is fair . . .

LOLA

When we drink!

ALL

Glorious wine, we hail your power, etc.

ALFIO (*enters*)

Happy Easter, good neighbors.

CHORUS

Neighbor Alfio, greetings!

TURIDDU

Won't you join us and drink with all
your neighbors?
(*pours a glass of wine*)
Here is your glass.

ALFIO (*respingendolo*)

Grazie. Ma il vostro vino io non
l'accetto,
Diverrebbe veleno entro il mio petto!

TURIDDU (*getta il vino*)

A piacer vostro!

LOLA

Ahimè! che mai sarà?

ALCUNE DONNE (*a Lola*)

Comare Lola, andiamo via di qua.
(*tutte le donne escono conducendo
Lola*)

TURIDDU

Avete altro a dirmi?

ALFIO

Io? nulla!

TURIDDU

Allora sono agli ordini vostri.

ALFIO

Or ora!

TURIDDU

Or ora!
(*Alfio e Turiddu si abbracciano. Turiddu morde l'orecchio destro di Alfio.*)

ALFIO

Compare Turiddu, avete morso a
buono.
(*con intenzione*)
C'intenderemo bene, a quel che pare!

TURIDDU

Compar Alfio, lo so che il torto è mio;
E ve lo giuro nel nome di Dio
Che al par d'un cane mi farei sgozzar,
Ma—s'io non vivo, resta abban-
donata—
Povera Santa! lei che mi s'è data.
Vi saprò in core il ferro mio piantar!

ALFIO (*freddamente*)

Compare, fate come più vi piace;
Io v'aspetto qui fuori, dietro l'orto.

(*esce*)

TURIDDU (*va a Lucia*)

Mamma, quel vino è generoso, e certo
Oggi troppi bicchier ne ho tran-
cannati--
Vado fuori all' aperto.
Ma prima voglio che mi benedite
Come quel giorno che partii soldato.
E poi, mamma, sentite
S'io non tornassi—voi dovrete fare
Da madre a Santa, ch'io le avea giurato
Di condurla all'altare.

LUCIA

Perchè parli così, figliuolo mio?

TURIDDU

Oh! nulla! È il vino che m' ha sugge-
rito!
Per me pregate Iddio!
Un bacio, mamma, un altro bacio,
addio!
(*l'abbraccia ed esce precipitosamente*)

LUCIA (*disperata correndo in fondo*)

Oh Turiddu?! che vuoi dire? (*entra
Santuzza.*) Santuzza!

SANTUZZA

(*getta le braccia al collo di Lucia*)
Oh! madre mia!
(*si sente un mormorio lontano*)

DONNE (*correndo*)

Hanno ammazzato compare Turiddu!
(*tutti gettano un grido*)

Cala precipitosamente il sipario.

ALFIO (*refusing him*)

Thank you! But I cannot accept your
    wine.
It might turn into poison inside my
    stomach!

TURIDDU (*throwing away the wine*)

If that's your pleasure . . .

LOLA

Dear God, what do you mean?

WOMEN

Good neighbor Lola, this is no place
    for us.
(*They go out, taking Lola with them.*)

TURIDDU

Have you anything further to tell me?

ALFIO

I? Nothing!

TURIDDU

Very well then. I'll be ready when you
    want me.

ALFIO

Right now!

TURIDDU

Why not?
(*Alfio and Turiddu embrace; Turiddu
    bites Alfio's right ear.*)

ALFIO

Neighbor Turiddu, I gladly accept your
    challenge.
            (*meaningfully*)
I think we have a perfect understand-
    ing.

TURIDDU

Wait, Alfio. I know that I have
    wronged you.
I must confess it, as God is my witness.
My sins are great, and I deserve to die.
Yet, if you kill me,
If I leave this world today,
She will be forsaken, my poor Santuzza,
She who was so trusting, she whom I
    abandoned,
I'll plunge my dagger in your heart
    today!

ALFIO (*coldly*)

My friend, what's the use of all this
    talking?
I'll be waiting for you behind the
    orchard. (*He goes off.*)

TURIDDU (*goes to Lucia*)

Mamma, I'm giddy . . . had one too
    many . . .
My head is whirling . . . I'll take a
    walk till I feel better.
I will walk in the orchard.
But first, dear Mamma, let me have
    your blessing,
As when I left you to be a soldier.
And listen! Mamma . . . please listen . . .
If I am destined never to return, pro-
    mise me, dear mother,
To help my poor Santuzza.
Love her and protect her as if she
    were your daughter.
Give me your promise.

LUCIA

What do you mean, Turiddu?

TURIDDU

Oh nothing! The wine has filled my
    head with folly.
Oh pray that God forgive me!
A kiss, dear Mamma——one more.
    Goodbye!

(*embraces her and goes out hastily*)

LUCIA
(*running desperately to the back*)

Turiddu? I am frightened!

        (*Santuzza enters.*)

Santuzza!

SANTUZZA
(*throwing her arms round Lucia*)

Mamma . . . oh Mamma!

    (*A tumult is heard from afar.*)

WOMEN (*running in*)

They've killed Turiddu!

(*A scream of terror from the crowd.*)

The curtain falls swiftly.